HORSES

Christopher Blazeman

Table of Contents

If You Were a Horse   3

All About Horses   6

How Horses Live   14

Horses at Work   20

Glossary   24

If You Were a Horse

Have you ever wished you were a horse?

If you were a horse, you would run like the wind.

You would have a long tail and mane.

You would be powerful and strong.

Oh, how wonderful to be a horse!

All About Horses

Horses are beautiful animals with strong muscles.

A horse can easily carry a person on its back.

A horse's powerful legs can run far and jump high.

Horses are fast, too. They are one of the fastest animals in the world. People like to watch horse races and guess which horse will run the fastest.

Horses come in many colors.
They can be black, white, brown,
gray, red, yellow, or more.
Sometimes they are two or three
colors at once.

A white spot at a horse's eye level or above is called a **star**. Any white mark below its eyes but above its nostrils is called a **strip**.

id you know that a zebra is type of horse?

Some horses have spots. Some horses have stripes. Some have both, and some have none.

Horses can be tall or short. Many horses are taller than people, but some horses are very small.

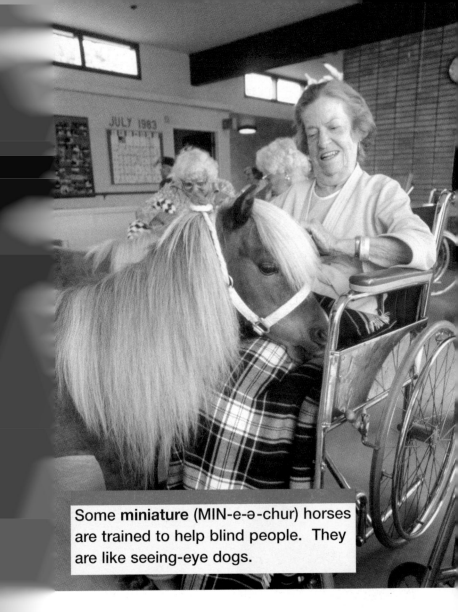

Some **miniature** (MIN-e-ə-chur) horses are trained to help blind people. They are like seeing-eye dogs.

A **miniature** horse may be ly two feet tall!

No matter their size, all horses have the same body parts. They are called **points**. Here are some of a horse's points.

Tail

A horse has only one toe on each foot. Each toe is covered by a horny hoof.
A **horseshoe** is used to protect the hoof.

A **muzzle** is a horse's jaw and nose. The **withers** is the ridge between a horse's two shoulder bones.

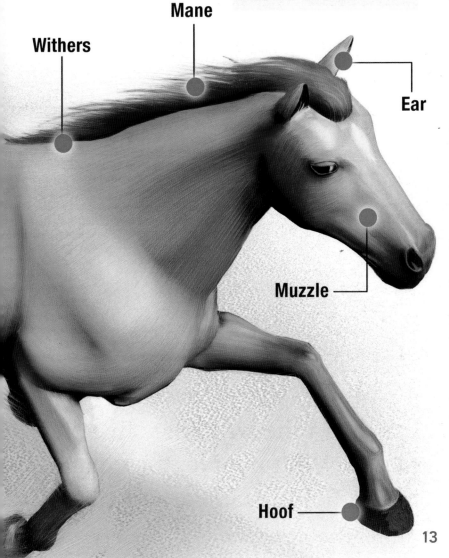

Mane

Withers

Ear

Muzzle

Hoof

How Horses Live

Horses live all over the world. In the wild, they live on plains. With people, they may live in fields, stables, and corrals.

Since they are so active, horses are big eaters. They eat plants. They especially like grasses and grains and sweet treats like apples and sugar cubes.

There are seven
million horses in the
United States.

A **stallion** is a male horse. A
female is a **mare**. Horse babies
are **colts** if they are boys and
fillies if they are girls. All horse
babies are called **foals**.

A mare nurses her foal to feed it. She keeps her foal near her while it is growing.

She also protects her foal. If there is danger, she will kick or bite anything that may harm her baby.

A horse's eyes are on the side of its head. Because of this, a horse can see almost everywhere around itself without turning its head. It can also see two different things at once, because each eye sees something different.

One thing a horse cannot see is whatever is right in front of its head! So, a horse can not see the food it eats.

Horses at Work

Horses have been helping people for thousands of years. They make people's lives easier by doing the hard jobs.

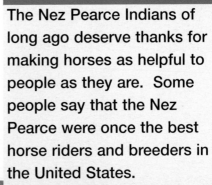

The Nez Pearce Indians of long ago deserve thanks for making horses as helpful to people as they are. Some people say that the Nez Pearce were once the best horse riders and breeders in the United States.

Some horses pull wagons and farm machinery. Some work for the police. Some work in the circus. Some help cowboys ride the range.

Throughout time, people have needed horses to help them.

Many people say that dogs are people's best friends. But horses may be even more important.

Glossary

mare and foal

hoof

stallion

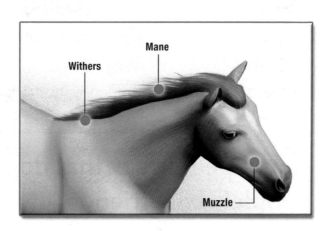

withers   mane   muzzle